Stephen Cherry is Dean of Ki… lications include *Barefoot Dis…* *humility* (the Archbishop of ~~Canterbury~~ ~~s Lent Book, 2011~~, *Barefoot Prayers: A meditation a day for Lent and Easter*, *Healing Agony: Reimagining forgiveness* and *Beyond Busyness: Time wisdom for ministry*.

For James: thinker, teacher and friend

BAREFOOT WAYS

*Praying through Advent,
Christmas and Epiphany*

Stephen Cherry

First published in Great Britain in 2015

Society for Promoting Christian Knowledge
36 Causton Street
London SW1P 4ST
www.spckpublishing.co.uk

British Library Cataloguing-in-Publication Data
A catalogue record for this book is available from the British Library

ISBN 978–0–281–07318–4
eBook ISBN 978–0–281–07319–1

Typeset by Graphicraft Limited, Hong Kong
Manufacture managed by Jellyfish
First printed in Great Britain by CPI
Subsequently digitally printed in Great Britain

eBook by Graphicraft Limited, Hong Kong

Produced on paper from sustainable forests

Contents

———•◦•———

Contents

PREPARATION (introducing the Great 'O' Antiphons)

CHRISTMAS EVE

THE 12 DAYS OF CHRISTMAS

January

Contents

SEEING

CARES

Contents

FLOURISHING

Introduction

————— ◦•◦•◦ —————

In the northern hemisphere, December and January are the darkest months of the year. Yet they host four Christian festivals of light: Advent, Christmas, Epiphany and Candlemas. Like all good festivals, these are not over in a day, but are short seasons which, in the case of Advent and Epiphany, can helpfully be subdivided.

In this collection I offer a meditation, poem or prayer for each day of the two-month period. The style of the pieces reflects the poem-prayers gathered in *Barefoot Prayers: A meditation a day for Lent and Easter*.[1] That collection was subdivided into even weeks. The Advent to Candlemas cycle doesn't map on to the calendar in the same way, and so the subdivisions are necessarily uneven.

Advent is divided into three periods. The introductory few days explore the fundamental Christian idea that God calls out to ordinary people who are part of the real world, and who sooner or later come to realize that they are sinners in need of a friend. The second subdivision explores the spirituality of time. There are good theological reasons for this – the Advent season reminds us that time belongs to God – but there are practical reasons too. For many of us this can be such a busy time that the things that take time and require patience can all too easily be squeezed out in the rush. There then follows a sub-season of eight days based on an ancient liturgical practice, which I explain in the introduction to that section.

---

[1] London: SPCK, 2013.

Christmas is just around the corner, but before it comes Christmas Eve. I have taken the view that this is a unique day, and so give it a whole subsection of its own. The 12 days of Christmas follow – and what days they are, moving quickly on from the humble joy of the word made flesh to the remembrance of the martyrdom of Stephen the deacon and the massacre of all the young boys in the Bethlehem district at the hands of the murderous Herod. The celebration of the turn of the year has become such an important secular festival that it is, I feel, more important to explore its spirituality than to refer to the ecclesiastical calendar on those days.

Epiphany is a longer, less intense season than Christmas, and one that gives more scope to the creative imagination to make a new map. So I have divided it into three sub-seasons: the first focus is on 'Seeing', an obvious Epiphany theme, but then suggest the theme of 'Cares' followed by 'Flourishing'. My intention here is to offer a simple narrative shape to a form of Christian development which begins with seeing, leads on to caring and ends in flourishing.

Candlemas brings the collection to a close, but that beautiful celebration is also disturbing. And so, just as we end, any naive optimism about pleasantly flourishing is removed and we are left, not enjoying the wonder of a church filled with candles, but nursing the wound in our hearts caused by old Simeon's words to the young mother, Mary. And so it is that we come not to closure, but to a reorientation towards the mysteries that will unfold at Easter.

Most of the pieces in this collection were written during 2014. As providence would have it, that was a year of travel and transition for me, and the imprint of impressions in different places is evident from time to time in some of the meditations. I will not spell that out here, but I do wish to acknowledge with heartfelt gratitude the support and spiritual companionship of former colleagues in the Diocese of Durham and at the incomparable Durham Cathedral, as well as of my new colleagues at King's College, Cambridge. And I extend my thanks to those who helped me with my various travels, enabling me to make of my journeys to Canada, Shetland, Hong Kong and Virginia genuine *visits*,[2] and friends who have supported my spiritual journey and encouraged me to write, especially Dame Laurentia Johns OSB and Sheryl Shenk. I have dedicated the collection to my son James, who crowned all the joys of a wonderful year by marrying Carrie on an auspicious day in July.

---

[2] In *Barefoot Disciple: Walking the way of passionate humility* (London: Continuum, 2010) I distinguish between a 'trip' and a 'visit'. A visit is an encounter in which there is openness to newness, learning, a sense of the strangeness of the self and, as a result, spiritual learning.

INTRODUCING ADVENT

———◆◆◆———

Advent affords the annual opportunity to begin again the journey of faith called Christianity. If we stay close, we will be transported by the memory of grace not simply to Christmas but through and beyond that to the new life promised and fulfilled at Easter and the vision of God that is sketched in the great post-Easter festivals of Pentecost and Trinity.

Such is the sweep of the ever-circling Christian year. Close up it can seem like a journey, a guided and nicely propelled transition from here to there. The truth however, is less easy. We are called, invited, drawn from the limits of what we have become towards and into the glory of what God is.

Some religions, and some versions of Christianity, set the journey from the old, unenlightened, unsaved self to the fullness of life with and in God as a once-and-for-all-time event. Those who follow the Christian year with faithful seriousness, on the other hand, recognize that not only is our spiritual transition at best partial and incomplete, but that as we ourselves become older through the passing of time, so we can continue to fall away from God. In other words, one reason for subjecting ourselves to the disciplines and rhythms of the

Christian year is that we respect (albeit grudgingly) the power of sin, and know that we are sinners both in theory and in fact.

So it is that these Advent meditations and prayers begin with two strong themes: calling and humility. There is no Christian spirituality without calling. 'You did not choose me, I chose you,' said Jesus to his followers in John's Gospel. Those words ring true to his disciples in this and every age.

And there is no Christian discipleship without humility. Christianity invites us to place our feet securely on the ground, to favour realism over idealism, to be practical in our purposes, and to limit abstract thinking to those areas of life where it facilitates engagement rather than distracts from it. Humility means engaging with the created world as it is – hence the poem-prayer about the bird-feeders. It also means being realistic about our limits, faults and failings.

It is traditional to see Advent as a time of repentance, but repentance only makes sense if we genuinely and sincerely see ourselves as sinners. For many people today, this is neither obvious nor straightforward. Oddly, we need to think and pray our way into an understanding of our own sinfulness. This, too, is spirituality and journey. And it is not only possible but wise because our Lord Jesus Christ is the ultimate friend of sinners.

Such, at least, is the beginning of our story, our journey, our common pilgrimage of faith.

A prayer before beginning

God the Almighty, from before the dawn of time you were preparing the way for your people to return to their eternal home. Call us, we pray, from the depths of our bewildered uncertainty, open our ears to the strains of your voice, and draw us from the toil of our earthbound cares to the delights and purposes you have prepared for us in our beloved Jesus Christ.

1 December

The God who calls

O God, you call us from the
plenitude of our troubles and the
plethora of our fears.

Give us courage as we
see the fragility of the path we must
tread, the openness of the landscape we must
cross, the length of the journey we must
begin, the darkness of the sky
under which we must travel.

Find us when we are lost,
guide us when the way is not
clear;
comfort us as we embrace
uncertainty,
confident only
in your
voice, calling from afar.

Ever-calling God,
help us to hear,
help us to follow,
help us to travel
and help us, one day,
to arrive.

2 December

Advent wreath

As I hang a wreath on my door, or blend
evergreens at the feet of candles
I wonder ...

I wonder about circles
and straight lines.
I wonder about eternity
and time.
I wonder, though this sounds grand, about the
purpose of my life.

Am I basically on a journey,
going from here to there?
Am I on a circular tour,
repeating experiences
again and again?
Am I ascending,
like the elegant flame at the candle's head,
or descending – like molten wax?

The years go forward,
The years circle round.

Do I ascend?
I may, I think, one day.
But first I descend:
like leaves, like water,
like wax, like Christ.

As I hang my wreath on the door, and blend
evergreens at the feet of candles,
I learn this:
my priority is
humility.

3 December

Feeder

Now the leaves have gone
they are more visible,
more vulnerable too,
the birds of garden, hedge and tree.

Filling the feeder takes on
an aspect of duty;
it is a lifeline for
the birds of garden, hedge and tree.

What better when sitting alone
than to await their flurry
in flocks, or as one or two,
the birds of garden, tree and hedge.

As the short days shorten, and
the long nights lengthen, teach me
the grace of looking,
   the grace of listening,
     the grace of being,
       the grace of loving,
        the grace of seeing
Thy fragile beauty,
so close at hand.

4 December

A prayer of the poor in spirit

I am awake today, alert and conscious
in a new way.
I think this is good, but
it is not comfortable.

I am aware, right now, that
I am a sinner among sinners.
This ordinary revelation shocks me
afresh; though I have had it many times before.
The truth is this: the fellowship in which
I am most naturally at home is
not the communion of saints, but
the company of sinners. My sad solidarity is with the
not so good.

Help me to live with this truth,
and to stand with my true peers.

Help me to accept:
my faults and my failings,
   my mistakes and my errors,
      my responsibility for harm and hurt,
         my tendency to misjudge risk,
            my inclination to judge others,
               my poverty of spirit.

Help me to seek forgiveness,
distasteful though the prospect seems.

Help me towards honesty,
and give me some of the humility I lack.

Let my life change, from the
inside out.
Free me from
the tangle of sin, but not,
I pray,
from the company of my fellow sinners.

5 December

Friend of sinners

Friend of sinners,
Be with those who wander:
  be with those who stray.
Be with all who fall short of their potential:
  with all who let themselves down.
Be with those who speak hurtful words:
  with those who needlessly inflict pain.
Be with all who nurse a grudge:
  with all who withhold their warmth.
Be with those who push themselves forward to receive credit
    that should fall on others:
  with all who defraud, cheat or steal.
Be with all who fail to speak out:
  all who pass by on the other side.
Be with those who undermine, malign or defame:
  those who bad-mouth others from spite.

Friend of sinners,
Be with those who stray:
  teach us all to repent.

6 December (St Nicholas)

Generosity

Generous God, ever sharing of yourself, ever flowing
from the eternal fountainhead, ever giving
the grace that heals and restores, that forgives
and renews, help me to become
a person of
generosity.

I do not pray that you would fill or satisfy me
with your grace, nor that you would enfold or
encompass me with your love.
Wash me, rather,
propel me,
challenge me and
send me;
involve me in your mission of love to
all and for all.

Fulfil me, I pray,
yes, I do pray for that, but fulfil me only
as I
share in the flow of your grace.

TIME

People today are obsessed with time. For many the problem is that there is not enough of it and they find themselves busy, stressed, rushed and overworked. For others, time hangs heavy and has become a torment. 'I'm bored' is the regular protest of the young, exacerbated perhaps by the nanosecond excitement that they enjoy through their high-tech toys.

But for the very elderly, those who can no longer enter into the fray of busyness that passes for meaningful life today, time is also a burden. Many are hoping not for a new excitement or a new distraction, but for the actual end. Having reached an age that would have astonished their own parents, and now finding themselves tired of life, they long for a release. 'How long, O Lord' is the prayer of many in their last years.

Human concern about time is not a new thing. The Christian tradition is cross-hatched with both impatience and the instruction to *wait*. And it's the waiting that matters.

Waiting is a fundamental aspect of Christian living. Indeed, you might even say that the whole of Christian spirituality and ethics is about what you do while you wait. But waiting is not about being passive. It is about acting in a way that is realistic about the actual capacity we have to make a difference.

And that is often less than we think, which is where the true pain of waiting sets in.

Waiting is always a reminder of the extent to which we *cannot* control things as much as we would like.

For many of us today it is very difficult. Some have suggested that people nowadays are addicted to control in the same way that an alcoholic is addicted to drink. Fr Anthony Ciorra has set out a 12-step process of spiritual development based on the famous 12 steps of Alcoholics Anonymous, precisely to help people overcome this crippling addiction to control. While insightful, it is sad that he has had to do this. The Christian calendar exists to make the point that all time belongs to God. It is to say that whatever else we think we can do, we cannot hasten or shorten God's timing.

There is, of course, no such thing as time management. All you can do is organize yourself and adjust your ambitions to reality. Being busy isn't something that happens to you like the flu. It is a state of mind and life that has forgotten that we cannot control things as much as we would like.

Yet we are impatient to our core. We are impatient when we are selfish – wanting our gratification without delay. But we are impatient when we are high-minded too. We want an end of injustice – now. We want to know the full truth – now. We want conflicts to be reconciled – now. We want peace in our hearts – now.

One of the failings of Christian spirituality in the last hundred years is that it has not engaged deeply enough with people's desires and hopes for the present moment. It has over-intellectualized 'now' and, in the wake of existentialism, suggested that the point about 'now' is that it is decision time.

That is part of the truth, but it's not the whole truth. The truer truth regarding many of the present moments that we live through is that our decision, our action, is neither here nor there, because in so many ways, and in the face of so many realities, we are actually powerless. This is one of the reasons why we often feel wretched when we hear the news: because we can't change it or stop it happening again tomorrow.

At every level we resent our lack of control and feel that the world would be so much better if we had more power to run it ourselves. This unlikely theory is the conviction not of the wise but of the hubristic.

Accepting our limits is the first lesson in Christian spirituality. It's not the last word, but it is a word of Advent. The message is that time, like power, is in God's hands. Our task is to learn not how to take control, but how to *tell* God's time and to respond to God's power and grace.

And the way we do that is by learning how to wait.

7 December

Time's arrow

Time is an arrow, they say,
though none can tell us
who drew the bow.
Time's arrow flies like
Halley's Comet, Bede's bird.
Whoosh and it is gone;
it is past,
drawing me into its
slipstream
yet accelerating away,
drawing me on when I want to
stop,
speeding when I want to
slow,
taking the straight line when I want to
soar, spiral, swoop and
rest.

Whence have you come,
mercurial one?
Whither are you going,
constant one?
When will your journey be done,
intrepid one?

Answer me not, then,
silent one.
Go your own way,
and I will go mine
following the compass of God,
as you fly by.

8 December

The joy of time

Teach us to number our
hours, that we might live time
wisely.

Teach us to forget our
minutes, that we might live them
calmly.

Teach us to relish our
moments, that we might live them
joyfully.

Teach us to cherish our
lives, that we might live them
generously.

For our days and our
hours, our minutes and our
moments, are your gift to us.

And for that gift we offer our
eternal Alleluia and our endless
Amen.

9 December

Time passes

To me time never
passes by.
It passes through.
Through my mind, heart,
    guts.
It is I who stand
outside time.
Not time outside me.

I find time both corrosive and
adhesive.
Like sand, it wears away whatever it
passes across.
Not smoothing, alas, but
roughing, scoring and scouring,
savagely etching its
signature on
any sensitive
surface.

It's sticky, is time.
Not like wet sand, which clings to
whatever it passes,
more like a magnet
or a vacuum.
It draws things forward, pulls them

after itself.
Time pulls us out of shape:
the mind is drawn forward,
the gut repulsed,
the heart torn.

So here I am
in one gnarled yet taut bundle,
temporally challenged

until
I catch up with myself.

That takes real time.

It's what it's for.

10 December

Litany for time wisdom

That we might apply ourselves to work we have planned and
be open to unexpected calls on our time.
Lord of the day: **We give you our time.**

That we might exercise responsibility with care and remain
calm when challenged, threatened or rushed.
Lord of the day: **We give you our time.**

That we might appreciate the efforts of others, even when
they disappoint us.
Lord of the day: **We give you our time.**

That we might be good colleagues, collaborators and partners
to all with whom we share priorities.
Lord of the day: **We give you our time.**

That we might grow in our sense of vocation and help others
to open themselves to your call in their daily lives.
Lord of the day: **We give you our time.**

That we might reflect your love and kindness to all with
whom we meet or connect this day.
Lord of the day: **We give you our time.**

From Stephen Cherry, *Beyond Busyness: Time wisdom for ministry**

---

* Durham: Sacristy Press, 2012, <www.sacristy.co.uk>. Reproduced with kind permission.

11 December

Busy day

O God, my prayer for today must be brief.
I am squeezing it in.
My day is overcrowded.
I am running to stand still.
I have too much to do.
I feel that pressure behind my eyes.
I am rushing.
I am anxious.
I am missing things.
I am sure I am missing things – very important things,
    actually.
I am tired – but far from sleepy.

All this is me.
I would rather it were
not, but it is.

So this is my prayer – I am getting round to it now.
Quickly - this is my prayer:

Teach me this day . . .
to find time to play.
Put the smile on my face . . .
that comes from your grace.

There you are. That's my prayer.
Corny perhaps, but sincere.

And yet even that's too much.
Make it this:
O God, save me from
myself.

12 December

Today

Although things are going well,
I am troubled by discontent.

It troubles me, this trouble, but
I cannot root it out. The present
moment is like a cage from which
I am always scrambling to be free.
I am like a captive creature, burrowing
against the glass.

Help me to resist the pull of the past
and check the fascination of the future;
help me to be with the people who populate the present;
deliver me from the demons of discontent
and driven-ness. Let me embrace the very-ness of this very day,
this hour,
this moment.

Let me drop down
to the depths of now and
drink water from the well of the
moment.

13 December (St Lucy)

Lucia

Wreathed in darkness as
dank as a slow death,
your wick burns brightly,
fuelled by faith.

Martyr and victim,
child – determined beyond adult imagination,
simply stubborn for God.
Inspire us to see what
you saw:
the light in the darkness of
history's deepest well.

14 December

Yes

It is hard to say 'no', I'm told.
And yet that is not my problem.
'No' is a liberating, pleasing word,
for me. I love its power, and control.

'I will not' gives me a strong sense of me.
'No!' I thunder, and the lightning strikes,
brilliantly catastrophic.

It's 'yes' that sticks in my throat.
I fear it as I fear duty, commitment,
limit.

So let me pray for the courage, the
wisdom, the
hope, the
strength – yes, all these are needed –
to say 'YES'.

Let me learn how to live with the constraints it will bring.
Let my 'yes' be yes,
and my 'no' be
its servant.

15 December

Two lilies

Her finger traced the
line, while mouth and lungs
breathed the words to life.

It was the scent that
first invaded her intensity.
Lilies: so insistent
in the afternoon heat.

Then sound, of a sort.
Less than rustling,
more the whisper of wind,
the murmur of something light.
As close to silence
as sound might be.
Just enough to stop her tongue,
to hold her heart,
on Isaiah's improbable words.

A second passed,
a minute,
an hour,
a life:
as
silence
spoke and heard,
asked and answered,

accepted and affirmed.
And Ave and Amen
chimed one strong
chord of solid
humility.

She breathed again.
There was no other sound.
The fragrance remained. And
the lilies. Two.
Lying across each
other on the
bare, baked earth.

It was three o'clock.

PREPARATION
(introducing the Great 'O' Antiphons)

———◆·◉·◆———

Advent invites us to enter into the traditions of the past in order to engage more deeply with the present and to imagine the future in a more informed way. One Advent tradition with very deep historical roots is the idea of a season within a season from 16 or 17 December to 23 December. This is the season of the Great 'O' Antiphons. It sounds, and is, a bit technical, but it is also very simple to understand. And rather charming.

All it means is that when the monks and nuns of old were singing their daily evening prayers (a service called Vespers in the older tradition and Evensong in Anglican circles) they had a special phrase to include before and after they recited the Song of Mary, or Magnificat. This tradition continues today in monastic houses, together with some churches and cathedrals. Each antiphon is based on one of the titles of the Messiah and each refers to one of Isaiah's prophecies concerning the Messiah. These titles are familiar to many Christians who have never heard of antiphons or Vespers or even visited a monastery, from the hymn 'O come, O come, Emmanuel'.

At Durham Cathedral there is a description of the life of the pre-Reformation Benedictine monastery called 'The Rites of Durham'. From these we learn that it was the duty of one of the senior or office-holding monks to recite one particular antiphon. One can easily imagine how this led to the idea that each office holder (they were known as 'obedientiaries') was deemed to have his own special day. We also learn that not only did the obedientiary say or sing that antiphon in the great church, they also had duties afterwards in the nice warm monastic common room – the 'calefactory'. This was the custom of the obedientaries 'keeping their O'.

The first duty was, of course, to say or sing the antiphon, but the second was to host a party in the calefactory. A little research reveals that the monks had some fun with this idea of keeping their 'O' in the days before Christmas. Who kept their 'O' on the day of the root of Jesse? The gardener. Whose turn when it was King of the Nations? The Provost. And on what day should the treasurer keep his 'O'? 'O key of David', of course.

From this I learn two things. First, that the 'O' antiphons have always been something to spark the wit and the imagination of Christians. And second, that the pre-Christmas party, so frowned upon by clergy of a certain ilk, has long been part of the actual life of the Church in the latter part of Advent. However, before this is taken as permission for uncontrolled self-indulgence, we should note that the Rites of Durham are careful to say that these little banquets of dates and raisins, ale and cakes, involved 'no superfluity or excesse but a scholastical and moderate congratulac'on among themselves'. And a further note adds that the occasion should be 'a very moderate one without superfluety'.

It is in this spirit that the following pre-Christmas meditations are offered.

16 December (O Sapientia)

Wise company

Although I know each day is new, that
there can be no subtraction of hours,
no going back,
it seems that I come once again to
the forest of middle life
aching with my lack of
wisdom.

I cannot see myself as wise,
yet there must be a path,
a step or two that I can take, without
stumbling and slipping stupidly
into the ditch.

And yet I fall
   again,
      and again.

Perhaps it's not wisdom I need but wise
companions, sensible friends to show me
where to place my feet,
and how to plant them firmly.
Good people who will shield me
from self-direction, and guide me
to the sweet
simplicity of your way.

17 December (O Adonai)

The Moses I love

This is the Moses I love.
Not the impetuous rebel.
Not the heroic liberator.
Not the angry law-giver.
Not the leader without a compass.
All these I respect, admire,
revere,
but none do I love.

This is the Moses I love:
the man at the burning bush,
turning aside, the captive
captivated by a great sight,
stopped in his tracks, stooping
to shift his sandals
quickly.

This is the Moses I love:
looking and listening,
arguing that he has no words,
lacking irony as well as
confidence and courage.

This is the Moses I love:
the man at the burning bush warming his heart
with mystery, boggling his mind
with truth, feasting his eyes on
unfuelled flame.

This is the Moses I love.
I will follow him as he stops.

18 December (O Radix)

The wisdom of plants

Teach me this day something of the
wisdom of plants:
their dignity,
their poise,
their capacity to feed themselves,
and refresh the air:
they make this planet
beautiful, green and habitable.

My mind wonders at their presence;
if they are absent, I miss them much.

My heart swells at their beauty,
colour, delicacy and profusion.
I love them as
nature's truest calendar.

Yet admirable and splendid as all this is,
I find no communion here. That
lies deeper.

My soul is at one with the hiddenness of plants:
their roots. My soul is my root:
the hidden me is radical.

Teach me this day to honour my roots:
the hidden, earth-clad, depths of myself.

Help me to hear the deep ancestral voice,
to feel the inherited wound,
to see again the congenital quirks in the glass.

Remind me this day of the hidden past, ever shaping
my visible present, that, inevitably unobserved,
it will continue to anchor and nourish me.

19 December (O Clavis)

Three keys

On the stone slab floor
stands the cold, white safe,
massive and impenetrable
without a key.

In my hand, smooth and sleek,
well worn and cared for,
that key sits snugly,
my servant, ready to turn

the deep and hidden lock
that keeps the door fast,
without which all strain
is frustration and waste.

For three keys I long,
for three keys I pray:
one for the future, one for the past,
one for this day.

The future is your book
closed, clasped and sealed,
locked firm for good,
on this you won't yield.

The past? The past was done
with the door open wide,
closing came after,
my choices fixed inside.

Here are my griefs,
in this metal box,
stacked like sardines,
salted with tears.

There is but one key
that I can possess,
the key of this day,
this moment, this hour.

That key is no less
than myself.
It is me.
And so I turn.

20 December (O Oriens)

Slant light

Lord of the dark, we wait for some sign of your coming.
It is indeed dark at this time,
and all signs of your light,
your glory, your hope are gone,
or hidden – I cannot tell.
All is dark.

Yet I call you, 'Lord of the dark',
believing in what I cannot see,
believing though I cannot see,
believing that, deep though this darkness is,
you are its Lord, believing
it will pass, believing that
its passing will be at your word.

Lord of the dark, we long for the light.
Not for the full light of summer noonday,
but the misted, slant light of winter dawn:
the light that brings hope.

Lord of the dark:
your darkness remains;
give us the hope that
hope will come.

Lord of the dark:
give us hope of hope.

21 December (O Rex Gentium)

Awkward angles

1

They treat us as clay indeed, the desire-makers:
we are plastic in their hands,
softer than putty or warm butter.

They fire us as earthenware pots that can
never be filled:
not transparent but porous, riddled with
pin-pricks through which contentment
runs out in rivulets.

2

The unwanted, odd-angled stone embarrasses the mason:
impossible to use in a foundation or wall. Undesired,
it waits on imagination and necessity:
the bridge, the strengthening arch, once
conceived, demand and prize the angular
one: it makes curve, construction and
connection possible.

3

O Thou, offering order and purpose to all:
come touch my imagination,
come transform my longing,
come transfigure my desire.

Let us be bridges, not walls,
and let our awkward angles be your
brightening materials.

22 December (O Emmanuel)

Stuck in traffic

Stuck in traffic on the motorway, or
between school and supermarket,
wiping warm mist from the windows
while glancing at my watch – such is the bleakness of
my midwinter,
punctuated not
by glimpses of sparkling hoarfrost, but by visits
to care home and hospital and those eye-searing supermarkets.

And lo, I learn that my heartbeat of
faith
has become the deep pulse of
doubt. Not energetically rejecting
the promise of soul, but diminished by the relentlessly inane.

Absence hangs heavy in the air, not eased, but
aggravated by the irritations of kitschmas.

Not that I mind the drink and the mayhem;
disorder and darkness seem to fit.
My problem is the falseness of the light, the
promise, the
cheer.

So come, so come, Emmanuel!
Embrace the poverty of my spirit, the
murkiness of my vision, the
thinness of my faith, and give
substance to my vapid hope and
diminishing love.

Be present, be present, O Emmanuel.
Be here.
Be now.
And save us all
from all this.

23 December (O Virgo Virginum)

Those feet

Angel's feet, doomed never to feel the soil,
silently sustain the grace of greeting,
treading the air without toil.

Mary's feet, in suspended gait,
one heel raised, toes pushed down,
poised, yet planted in given ground,
wait.

He will fly and she will walk
and walk and walk,
kneading body, earth and mind
into a basic trinity
of plodding, falling humankind,
pacing out with even stride – no Jacob, she –
the sand and straw and stone,
the dirt and dung and dust,
of ground made ready now
to take the print of Word made flesh.

CHRISTMAS EVE

———•◆•———

Christmas Eve is a strange day. Unique in atmosphere and meaning, it doesn't belong in the 12 days of Christmas. Yet it is not properly part of Advent either. Perhaps it needs to be divided: the morning given to Advent – for final preparations, the last-minute shopping or some wrapping – and the afternoon and evening to Christmas itself.

During the twentieth century the idea developed that Christmas begins at 3 p.m. on Christmas Eve. All over the world, radio sets are tuned to the BBC, often via local radio stations or the World Service. And from a silent chapel in Cambridge comes the trembling voice of a boy treble: 'Once in royal . . .'

Inside the chapel a thousand people are standing in quivering silence. They are uniquely aware of time – it is time at last, after all that queueing; and supremely aware of space – the sound is going out to all lands. People know that for the rest of their lives, wherever they might be, when they tune into this particular broadcast they will recall having been there. And when they tell others they will share stories of the remote spots in which they have heard this service, and the days of dark sadness it has illuminated. My own memories include once, when I was a curate, hearing the first part of the service on the car radio while driving to a hospital to visit patients in a stroke ward, then hearing the last part on the way home – the sadly incapacitated and soon-to-die stroke victims being enfolded, as it were, in the generous spirituality of that great and mysterious service. And so it is that the throng in the chapel will cast their minds to those listening across the world in places remoter, hotter and colder than we can normally manage to imagine.

What matters about Christmas Eve, of course, is the 'Eve': the time when light at last falls away and the darkness arrives. The cloak of darkness is precisely where the Christ-child will be born, not for reasons of secrecy or protection, but because the true light is gracefully drawn not to places that are pleasantly illuminated, but to the deepest darkness.

The Chapel of King's College, Cambridge, is remarkable in many ways, not least for its famous and distinctive acoustic properties – its sound is unique. But for the few who attend this service in the chapel itself, the play of light is even more affecting and significant.

The stained-glass windows of the chapel are huge, and if the day is sunny the chapel will be bright and beautiful at 3 p.m. An hour or so later the windows will be dark. Natural light will have departed. The flickering candles around the choir will appear much brighter, and they will form a pool of light which might pass for a huge cradle. And it is from here that the final resounding lesson (John 1.1–13) is read, from which the title of the next meditation is a quotation.

24 December (Christmas Eve)

And the darkness comprehended it not

As the sun slips the horizon
it barely transcended:

    degree by degree,
    inch by inch.

As the darkness rises
to black the great windows:

    colour by colour,
    pane by pane.

As the hoarfrost gathers
to glisten creation:

    blade by blade,
    twig by twig.

Let my prayer rise before you
as tranquil as incense:

    cloud by cloud,
    plume by plume.

Let my hands be uplifted
as gift and acceptance:

finger by finger,
palm by palm.

And let this night fall
with seismic thud

to be vanquished and healed
by the flint-flash of God.

THE 12 DAYS OF CHRISTMAS

Christmas is perhaps the Christian festival that most invites *stillness*. 'He came al so stille', as the ancient, anonymous poet puts it, 'as dew in Aprille'. This is why the nativity inspires such impressive artworks. The simple scene, whether it is of mother and child alone, or being visited by shepherds, or adored by magi, or just accompanied by animals, speaks of the calm and completeness of love.

Yet the incarnation of the son of God does not so much stop the clock as start the calendar. We cannot expect ourselves to note 'AD – Anno Domini' wherever we jot down the date, but every now and again we might do more to remember it. Poets have seen in the incarnation a land of death – and rightly so. More fundamentally, however, as well as more obviously, it is a birth.

There is in Christmas, then, a forward-looking dynamic as well as a contemplative stillness. This is reflected in the delightful and wise tradition of extending the feast of Christmas across 12 days. There is no need to find an excuse for a party at this time of year. The one day of Christmas is an inadequate container for the goodwill and cheer that Christmas rightly evokes.

And yet the calendar of the Church doesn't invite us to abide by the crib, gurgling at the baby or congratulating the parents, for very long. The second day of Christmas is not 'Boxing Day' but the 'Feast of Stephen' – the first martyr. We are in death country now, though Stephen's horrible stoning, a bloody death indeed, is depicted as a beautiful event in the Acts of the Apostles. There is no such aesthetic relief two days later when the slaughter of the Holy Innocents is recalled.

The celebration of the New Year has become a major secular festival, and provides occasions for recollection and rededication. For all the seriousness of the Christmas season, happiness and laughter are part of Christian spirituality, part of who we are in a deep as well as light and trivial way. And so too is folly. If the season of Christmas begins with the silence of holiness, it ends with the merry noise of foolishness. The Twelfth Night is the night of the jester, the fool: the one who mocks our pretence and helps us laugh our way to wisdom, gently shedding our pretences and goading us to open our eyes to the humbling birth of who we really are.

25 December (Christmas Day)

Feast of feasts

Joy of joys,
Gift of gifts,
Song of songs,
Heart of hearts,
Mind of minds,
Love of loves,
Hope of hopes,
Star of stars,
Light of light,
Child of child:
on this day of days,
bless our feast of feasts.

26 December (St Stephen)

The first stone

It's the baby's first breath that
elicits the mother's first
smile. The first sip of orange that
breaks the dawn of
taste. The first hint of coffee that
quickens the
will.

It's the child's first
step, the lovers' first
kiss, the first cut from the
cake, the first slice from the
loaf.

It's the first frost of
autumn, the first snow of
winter, the first flower of
spring, the first swim of
summer.

Yes, it's the first that makes the
memory.

They call me the first
martyr, the first
witness. But I was not the first
to testify. I was not the first
to see. I was not the first to put the Way into
words.

My witness was to inspiration
received, incarnation
understood. I had seen the Alpha, and lost all fear of the
Omega. But I was not first. I was among
many.

Yet this I know.
This I testify.
This is my
witness.

It's the first stone that strikes the hardest
blow, that takes away the
breath.

It's the first stone that shows the calculation of
cruelty, the determination of
fear, the damnation of
hate.

Let me speak of the reality of that first,
human-thrown,
rib-cracking,
heart-breaking,
story-ending,
stone.

Let me witness to that half pound of solid, air-borne
creation.

That was the stone, that first one, that finally fractured my
      shell of
self; that let my spirit fly
free.

Think not of me as the
first. Think of that
stone. And
rejoice.

27 December (St John)

The world would be too small

You were so frustrated that day,
and so were we. Our hands were sore, our backs
ached. 'Certainly it is accomplished,' we moaned.
It must be done. All had been said and
written.

We were expecting your nod, a shuffle of the
eyebrows, a silence followed by one of your multiple
affirmations: 'Yes, yes, yes, yes . . .
and yes.'

But no! You were insistent,
silently and stubbornly insistent. You
stood, arms stretched like wings, as if you were
landing on a high crag.
We sat, waiting for your dictation to begin. For the
words to flow.

In front of us your witness.
'The testimony of John,' it began. But
this was Baptist John, not Writer John. It was his and yours
but not yet fully yours.

'I must give more,' you said, 'one more grain of truth.' Then
the silence fell again, like mist on a mountain-top.

You swirled within it. You
champed and growled. You
walked in circles. You
ground your teeth. You
lost all sense of us with you.

You were struggling within, wrestling with some
unseen angel, some cruel angel
who gave you vision and desire
but no words. The word-angel had
departed, it seemed, leaving only
a deep demented clucking, a pre-verbal babbling.

Your winged tongue was
earth-bound at last.

We both shed a tear as we recalled the
eagle you truly are, those soaring flights
we had witnessed and recorded. That majestic
     control and supernal
synthesis that left you so deeply
drained. It was your death we anticipated that day.
We feared for your eternal silence.

When the first words
formed, we missed them. We failed to write.

'In the beginning,' you repeated.

'Genesis,' we thought. This could be a long day.

'In the beginning,' you repeated again. 'In the beginning
    was the *word*.'

We caught each other's eye, and started to write.

And you continued, arms still extended, 'and the
word was with God, and the word was
God.'

And so you
flowed, and so we
wrote, we wrote, *we*
wrote, 'the word became
flesh and dwelt among us'.

When you had finished, you let your arms
drop. You stood for a while and then sat. There were three of us,
sitting with your words.

After a while you began
to chuckle. 'The end! The end!' you
said. 'No! No!' we protested.
'Add this to the end,'
you insisted, still chuckling. 'Add this:
"If all was written, the world would be too
small for the books."'

Then you opened your arms wider than ever and
roared with laughter till the tears
drenched your straggly old beard. You
stood up, rather grandly as I recall, arms still outstretched:

'The world would be too small. The world would be too small.
Yes, yes, the world would be too small. Yes, yes, yes, yes . . .
and yes! The world would be too
small.'

28 December (Holy Innocents)

———————

Imagine not

She called it the day of which we do not
speak. My grandmother. She was there. One of the
youngest.

Hers was a girl, but they killed her
anyway. Herod's
men.

I don't know why she broke her vow
with me, but one day she spoke of that
unspoken day. She had been seventeen, as I was that
day she described the sound of their
coming; relived the hour of
sword and club; related the days of
lament. The sleepless
years.

Never have I seen such
sorrow. Never seen such bleakness of
eye. Never have I heard such a long, slow, deep, mournful
moan as slipped from her
soul after the
telling.

She died soon after. Closing the ranks of her
generation, sealing the sisterhood of death with
death.

As she went, her eye fixed mine. 'You know,' it
said. 'You know a
little.'

I replied in words which had been
long in coming. 'I have been there; I have imagined.'
I held her
hand.

She raised her head and fixed my eye again. I quailed
at the effort it cost her. She drew her last draught of
air then exhaled at me from the depths of her dying
lungs:

'Imagine it not!'

She fell back. Eyes open, but still.
I stayed with her as, one by one, the canyons above her
eyes, and bulbs below, calmed and sagged,
marking in their relaxation the death of her
memory.

I took a vow to kill my
imagination that day. Yet it
lives.

Let me be true to the truth
it tells.

29 December

Summer in winter

Summer in winter,
light in darkness,
presence in absence;

Cloud of charity,
mine of mercy,
river of grace;

Infinite intelligence,
fathomless wisdom,
boundless joy;

Be Thou my mind this day,
and let my heart be Thine.

30 December

Memories

It's reassuring when they come back.
'Flooding', we call it, greeting this
unbidden inundation of consciousness
as if it had no shadow.

But under the fallen leaves of memory,
thick piled and mulching on the winter earth,
lie forgotten moments,
never-to-be-recollected days,
whole books read,
entire outings,
complete personalities – school friends (who was it sat at
    that desk?),
as well as truths, details, proofs, routes, recipes and
punchlines.

I raise a grateful cheer for memory,
delighting daily in all that is recollected,
recalled, relived in reverie.

But my more grateful prayer is for
forgetting. I am glad to forget the humdrum and the
tedious. I am glad to forget my worst moments,
greatest embarrassments (as long as I can).
I am glad to forget disagreements and disputes,
spats and rows.

I am glad to forget so many things – I cannot recall –
so many things that are better left
under the mulch of my recollections.

Thank God, then, not only for
memories, but for the mind's kind
wisdom for forgetting.

31 December

Examen for the year's end

As the year's final sands fall swiftly
through the narrow hip of the glass,
teasing me that they are speeding up:

Let me find a wayside bench where I can
rest and reflect – just a few seconds
for each month of the year past.

Let me feel again the heart moments that
mattered most.

Let me think back to
before the problem was solved, the decision made.

Let me recall the faces and voices that
meant much, that cared for me,
drew me on, restrained me with love.

Let me be grateful for those who,
by giving me some unwittingly difficult word,
wounded and saved me.

Let me remember the places where
good things happened; where there
was refreshment, delight and social joy.

Let me recollect treats and feasts, visits and encounters.

Let me recall where radiance was.

Let me be grateful for the good days,
the good people,
the good times.

Let me visit once more the
shadows and shades of sad or benighted
minutes and days, the hours
when purpose was eclipsed,
the moments when I met
hostility with fear,
where uncertainty made me anxious,
when I took the opportunity for the cruel look,
the self-indulgent feeling, the times when
it was my sin that spoke.

Let me fly back over the
months, hovering where I should,
pinpointing grace and disgrace,
joy and woe, occasions when I have
done well or let myself down.

And all this not for the sake of the
past alone, though it deserves its proportionate honour or
    shame,
but for the joy of the present
yet to come.

1 January

Beatitudes for the New Year

Looking forward, I pray for
happiness; real, robust
happiness:
happiness that swells roundly with
wellbeing, while my ego thins to a trim
leanness.

Let me be happy when
reminded of my own inadequacies.

Let me be happy when
my actions are gentle.

Let me be happy when
I see a truth – or say one – heedless of consequences.

Let me be happy when
I turn from a mistake.

Let me be happy when
I see others flourish, especially my rivals.

Let me be happy when
others take the trouble to belittle or defame me, ridicule or
    bad-mouth me.

Let me be happy when
a loss reveals the depth of a love that might not have been.

Let me be happy when
my energy is spent.

Let me be happy when
a question arises which no one can answer.

Let me be happy when
giving and receiving.

Let me be happy to rejoice in all that is real.

And let my happiness bring only
happiness to others.

2 January

Laughter

There is a sound I know
more precious than any
other. Nothing
can force or contrive it,
nor can the ear ever be
fooled by fakes.

It is the sound of true
laughter. Unaffected and
unadorned, it comes to
greet the harmless absurd,
rushing irresistibly from head,
heart, lung and belly.

Here comes laughter,
fanning flames of fun,
warming souls,
melting brittle-boned
boundaries,
while wining and
one-ing us for good.

Let laughter my companion be,
and let it make of us
a company of friends.

Turn me from its lesser kin,
the nervous laugh,
the cruel sneer,
the knowing snort,
the nasty grin.

Calm my desire for more
mirth than I am due,
forgive my greed for
levity bought at another's expense.

Let laughter live, but let
me pay.
Let my pride and vanity write the
cheque that liberates the sour-sweet
tears.

Let laughter level us as
we rise together.
Freely absurd.
Absurdly free.

3 January

A prayer for many gifts

Give me, O Lord,
a calm soul and a clear head,
a broad mind and a generous spirit.

Give me,
a hunger for justice and a thirst for peace,
a passion for truth and a love of mercy.

Give me,
a painter's eye and a poet's tongue,
a saint's patience and a prophet's hope.

Give me,
a sage's wisdom and a fool's delight,
a pilgrim's purpose and an angel's content.

Give me,
a warm heart and a listening ear,
my true voice and a gentle touch.

4 January

Cross-purposes

Am I alone, I wonder, in being
torn by the dissonance of Christmas?

Am I alone, I wonder, in feeling
depleted by the festival?

Am I alone, I wonder, in longing
not for more, but for less
when the light of the word is beginning to
glow in the dark?

Am I alone, I wonder, in feeling
the spiritual magnetism of simplicity
at this time of long nights and fragile hopes?

Am I alone, I wonder, as I am achingly drawn
to profundity, and yet anguished by my own succumbing to the
barbed charms
of the superficial?

Am I alone, I wonder, when I feel
at cross-purposes with the world,
when I am disinclined
to meet its expectations?

No, I am not alone.
I am called.

5 January

———⋅•⋅•⋅———

Twelfth Night

It seems a matter of
witness to us
to retain our
cheer until this
night, when all around
hastened swiftly
on, after too many weeks of
booze and
bling.

Let contrary-wisdom
reign this night. Give us a
bean-king,
a lord of misrule,
a jester from the court
of the king of kings:
a fool of fools, no less,
that folly may reign an hour more.

True wisdom will come another day
star-gazing, gift-laden,
fooling one king, adoring the other,
teaching all the pathos of fear and pride.

Give us, we pray, the wisdom to wait on
wisdom's hour, and
the freedom to
fear nothing.

SEEING

————•◦•————

The short season of Christmas is followed by the longer one of Epiphany. The word sounds strange on English lips, and means 'manifestation'. It holds on to the idea that when Christ was visited by the magi he was revealed to them and thereby made known to the whole world. Liturgists tell us that the baptism of Christ and the miracle of water into wine at Cana can tell the same story, but it's the magi who define Epiphany.

It is remarkable, if not ironic, that this story is found in Matthew's Gospel. It is by far the most Jewish of the four, and often explains events in the life of Christ as the fulfilment of Scripture or prophecy. Scholars argue that it was written for a synagogue which became a church. This explains its opening verses: the genealogy of Jesus, showing him to be descended from Abraham. The story of the magi is more difficult to explain; there is not much else in Matthew about Jesus made manifest as Christ to those at a distance from the Jewish tradition. Indeed, the identity of Jesus is something of a mystery in Matthew (though less of one than in Mark). Peter seems to be the only one trusted to give a definitive answer to the question, 'Who do you say that I am?' (Matthew 15.16). That he does so at the

Roman city of Caesarea Philippi, which is the historic home of the pagan god Pan, is perhaps a hint, but it is a very subtle one. There is less subtlety at the very end of the Gospel, where the soon to be ascended Jesus tells his 11 disciples (some of whom even then doubted) to 'make disciples of all nations' (Matthew 28.19).

The question of what we see is an important and spiritual one. It's not quite the same as what we choose to look at – where we direct our attention – though that matters too.

Early Christian art was Jewish enough *not* to seek to give a likeness of Christ in visual form. The second commandment forbade it, and indeed the higher the theology of Christ that was held, the greater the offence in making an image would be.

None of this, however, stopped people in later centuries doing their theology through visual art, by creating images that, precisely because they do not pretend to represent, do communicate and reveal.

And so it is that our seeing matters, in both a real and a metaphorical sense. The visual world is God's world, and we can behold truth and glory, grace and peace in it. Like Rembrandt, we can see the luminescence of meaning set in the swirling, threatening darkness all around. Like him, and like the great Jewish teachers of old, we can see, or at least fancy we see, the very *shekinah* – the uncreated glow of glorious, holy presence in creation itself – with our ordinary eyes.

If we believe that 'Epiphany' is more than just an unlikely word to describe the visit of three kings, we must surely seek the manifestation of the glory of God wherever our eyes might lead us. There is nothing in the Christian story to suggest that it is more propitious to look in one place than in another. Rather, the invitation is constantly made to seek and to look with the eyes of faith. These are new and different eyes: eyes that have already been transformed – like the magi's – by the experience of being let down by the humanly powerful, and elevated by the extraordinary beauty of everyday holiness.

6 January (Epiphany)

The way of the wise

The wise had seen,
  seen doubly,
star and child.

The wise had worshipped,
  worshipped doubly,
bow and gift.

The wise had departed,
  departed differently,
another way.

7 January

A prayer for revelation

O hidden One,
O ancient of days,
O Lord of time and space.

O countenance of mercy,
O face of justice,
O prince of peace.

Reveal this day the glimpse of your glory
that will nourish me
in faith and hope.

Assure me kindly of your presence and love,
and fulfil your word, so that I can live
not only as your servant

but as your companion,
this day
and all my days.

8 January

Seeing God

If you want to know what it is like
to see God:

Imagine you are a
baby
looking at a breast.

Imagine you are a
sailor
looking at a whale.

Imagine you are the
moon
looking at the earth.

Imagine you are a
raindrop
looking at the sun.

Imagine you are
thistledown
looking at the breeze.

Imagine you are a
mirror
looking at a face.

Imagine you are a
breast
looking at a baby.

Imagine you are a
nail
looking at a hand.

And keep
looking.

9 January

—◆—

Before reading

As I sit down to read,
pick up a book,
and cast my eye to the clock,
bless me, I pray,
with carefree attention,
relaxed focus, and
restrained imagination
so that these words,
so carefully chosen,
crafted,
arranged and
edited
might seep into my eyes,
my mind,
my heart,
my soul.

Bless, I pray, this reading
time and
bless the author who troubled to write
that I might read.

10 January

Green

Lord of life, we thank you for green.
The many greens of your plants which fill us with joy and hope.
The light and gentle greens of new leaves on tall trees.
The deep greens of undergrowth.
The bright grassy greens of the meadows.
The rich, nutritious greens of the vegetable patch.
The dusky greens of fruits before they ripen.
The blacker greens of pine and spruce.

We praise you for all that green means to us:
for the green of inexperience and naivety,
for the green of Islam,
the green of environmental awareness and action.

Teach us to live well with green things.
Give us green minds and souls
and help us to see and know
and love you in all that is green.

11 January

Blue

Creator of all,
you made our planet blue with the water of the oceans.
And you made the sky, a canopy of
blue to brighten our days and lift our hearts.

Bless us through all that is blue,
all that reflects the mystery and wonder of sea and sky.

We praise you for dyes and paints that are blue –
light and dark,
deep and bright.
We praise you for the blue in mauve, purple
and violet.
We praise you for deep, dark blues in ancient art and on
printed page, blues which draw
our eye and mind and will,
which invite us to contemplate infinite depth.

We remember before you blue glass,
warning us of toxicity within.
Help us to take care whenever near danger. Let us use toxins
lightly.

We love you for music that is blue, stretching our sadness and
liberating our longing.

O Thou, who made a blue planet and a blue sky:
open our eyes,
open our hearts,
open our souls
to all that is blue out there,
and all that is blue within,
that we may be blessed by blue.

12 January

Red

Presence in the burning bush, we thank you for all that is red.

For the hidden redness of our hearts, and blood that
seeps from us, reminding us of vulnerability, wound and
 sacrifice.

For the red we see in bold petal, brilliant feather and exotic leaf.
For the red of sky in warning and delight.

We praise you for the signal red of danger present:
stopping us, protecting us, altering and alarming us.

Sing alleluia for the red of rust: hinting at time,
 checking our pride, slowing us down.
Sing alleluia for the red of fire, ember and flame,
 glowing and licking, dancing and terrifying.
Sing alleluia for the martyrs whose blood flowed,
 whose hearts broke, whose limbs melted into flame.

Red, Lord, the colour of your spirit: let it flow within us,
through us,
from us.

Let it touch us, inspire us,
inflame us.

Let our red be your passion,
and your passion be our
purpose.

CARES

Wouldn't it would be nice if a glimpse of the glory of God brought to our hearts and minds that peace which passes all understanding, and settles us down for enjoyable contemplation of all that is lovely and good?

Alas, the impact is often the exact opposite. Once you have a sense of God, contentment is yet more difficult to find. This is not because God teases us with moments of fulfilling presence followed by weeks, months and years of apparent absence, like some divine parent playing a very long game of 'peek-a-boo'. Certainly many experience something just like that: aridity of spirit, dryness in prayer, the famous 'dark night of the soul'.

What I have in mind here, however, is something more ordinary and yet perhaps more honourable. It is discontent driven by compassion, the 'cares' of the sensitive soul.

That Advent, Christmas and Epiphany should issue in 'cares' ought not to be surprising to someone who has witnessed Christian faith in action. Caring is a fundamental aspect of Christian character; and to care is integral to authentic discipleship and the basis of all authentic ministry. And if mission is not caring, it is not mission.

To be an 'uncaring Christian' is to introduce real tension into your soul. Once the glory of God has been glimpsed, and once it is understood to be made flesh in a person of vulnerability who would be killed because of the threat his healing, exorcising and teaching life was to the religious authorities, then the option of 'not caring' has been decisively and permanently sealed off. To try *not* to care as a Christian is to try not to be a Christian. It is certainly to lack Christian integrity.

Yet many today seek integrity. They hope for it for themselves and search for it in those who aspire to influence or leadership. People want and need authenticity. They experience an existential need to encounter the real deal. Only when they find it will they accept authority. And in Christian life, faith and spirituality this means that caring, and its twin, compassion, have a non-negotiable priority.

Care and compassion connect with spirituality and faith in prayers of intercession. In public worship these have been styled in many different ways down the years: litanies, biddings, collects, and comprehensive paragraph prayers. A visit to a local church today will probably mean hearing such prayers led by a person who has listened anxiously to a news broadcast, consulted an official list of who should be prayed for, been informed about who from the congregation is unwell, and noted the names of the recently departed. All these have their place, and have the advantage of rhythm – a very helpful dynamic in prayer.

Such prayer can, to the modern ear, be a little worthy and perhaps a tad dull. It is rarely beautiful or rich enough to connect with the deeper subtleties of the spirit, in response to which some people respond gratefully to Prayer Book or Shakespearian language, while others delight in the unpolished words that can be offered extempore; yet others find that prayer is just a matter of more and more words until someone adds some music or provides some visual images to help the spirit along.

There is no doubt that we should pray our cares, or that there is endless scope to expand their range or to deepen the intensity of our God-directed longing, that others might be healed, comforted, enriched and glorified by a divine touch. We cannot, of course, organize any such thing. Nonetheless, the habit of our tradition is that we should pray our cares regularly and faithfully, entrusting others to the love and mercy of the one we believe to be most loving and most merciful. If to that habit we add appropriate imagination, creativity and art, we may have taken a positive, if vulnerable, step along the Way.

13 January

Winter fuel

As I move across the room to the fire – electric,
gas, solid fuel – whatever it is – so I remember
those colder than me this day.

As I ladle soup from the pan, I remember those
whose bowls are dry.

As I warm my meal, I remember those
whose food is cold.

As I queue at the shop, I remember those
who long for frustration like this.

God of the cold, the poor,
the hungry . . .
be with those who are most nearly yours this day.
And be with us all,
that together we might turn the tide of history
towards the justice
your love demands
and for which we so lazily long.

14 January

———•◆•———

Cold day

It's not the dark of the pre-dawn that
disappoints my rested heart.
It's the cold of the day to come.

I bring, or so it seems to me, only
a little spring,
a little hope,
a little kindness,
a little love,
a little invitation to joy.

I make my gift small,
too tiny to matter, or to threaten
hurt or harm.
And yet it is greeted with a
frost that makes me shudder.

Help me, gracious one, to stay warm in the cold,
to hold hope against the dull despair that keeps closed
the curtains of the heart.

Help me to walk slowly into the fog of
human sadness, to step gently on the ice-filmed mud of
discontent, to wade calmly through the sodden soil of
desolation.

And let me do it with the pulse of
joy in my veins; and the breath
of hope in my lungs.

The day is dark and cold. Let me live
light, let me give warmth. Let me live
joy, let me give hope.

15 January

The hot

I pray for those exposed to overwhelming
heat this day:
those who live in shanty towns or slums in humid and
hot areas of overlarge cities;
those traversing great plains and deserts;
those exposed to cloudless skies;
those working in unventilated spaces
– factories, workshops, mines;
those breaking their backs in fields, whether
ploughing, sowing, tending or harvesting;
those working close to furnaces and fires;
those living in places that never cool at night
and where rest is ever restless;
those running a fevered temperature;
those wearing heavy protective clothing.

I pray for all who wait in vain for
some
relief and refreshment
from enervating heat.

I pray for them all:
that their sweltering lives may not be lonely,
that their hope might be strong,
and that every opportunity to improve their
quality of life might be taken.
And I pray that my own actions will be
such as only to improve their chances
of enjoying life
at a liveable temperature.

16 January

Before the morning watch

It's one thing not to be able to fall asleep;
that's bad enough:
circling thoughts,
irritation,
lack of calm.
Energy? Yes, some, but not enough.
Circling thoughts? Yes, circling thoughts.
This is not worse but it is different and desperate.
Sleep has come, refreshed profoundly it seems,
yet also incompletely – and departed
before dawn
like a greyhound from a trap.

Oh, how I miss the warm, well-paced
breathing of just a moment
ago; the dream-free or dream-laden
(I will take either) cinema
darkness of my unbusy
mind.
Yet here I am, awake and
alert, yet
vacant, ready, yet
knowing above all else that it is not yet
time.
Re-calm me, Holy One, in this unplanned,
pre-dawn vigil.
Reclaim me.

Keep me from the
panic I begin to feel as the hours
take shape. Form in me a prayer of presence
and hope, of longing
and good desire. Let me see my day,
my life,
my plans,
not projected forward with anxious
uncertainty, but framed as
uncertain ventures to come.
And let me embrace them.

Give me hope, Holy One.
Give me love, Holy One.
Give me grace, Holy One.
Let me delight in the calm of this
not-yet day. Let my soul fly to you
at this small hour
before the morning watch.

17 January

———————

Stamina

God of endurance, I pray for
stamina this day.
There is no task for me to rush at. There is nothing I can
quickly achieve, nothing that can easily be ticked off my list.
I must work slowly,
methodically,
patiently.
I must work diligently, not succumbing to the temptation to
      digress:
a temptation I expect to face
three or four times an hour.

Keep me focused.
Keep me patient.
Keep me committed.

Help me to pace myself,
taking breaks and remaining fresh.

Help me to remember that what I do today may not be
much; but that it might be crucial – when seen with
the wisdom of retrospect.

Give me even today a hint of my future
hindsight. Let it shape my
judgements, my
diligence, my
endurance;
let it give me
stamina.

18 January

————••••————

Difficult people

Lord of all, I pray this day for difficult people:
   those who get under my skin and irritate me;
    those who discomfort and disconcert me;
     those who simply see the world differently.

Help me to live with the tension this creates.
Help me to harness the energy it can liberate.
Help me to find beauty in discord.
Help me to adjust and accommodate to the strengths and
   virtues of others.
But help me, too, Lord of all,
to be robust when I need to be:
to know where to draw the lines of dignity;
to know how to resist those who are not only difficult,
   but destructive,
not only difficult,
   but devious,
not only difficult,
   but determined to impose.

Help me, Lord, to discern the cause of difficulty in difficult
   people
and to be deliberate,
direct and
discriminating in response,
emulating, where possible, the prayer-filled
decisiveness of your Son, Jesus Christ
our Lord,
the most difficult person of all.

19 January

—————•◦•—————

A pastor's prayer

Open my eyes,
open my ears,
open my wisdom,
that I might see, hear
and in some way understand
the people I encounter this day.

Let me connect with their energy
and pain,
their purpose
and intention.

Let me, without fuss or fascination,
attend simply and deeply, noticing
just enough.

Let me look and listen with
sufficient calm,
    sufficient kindness,
        sufficient humour,
that something might unfold in their depths;
    that something might be eased;
        that something might be freed.

Let my looking,
    let my listening,
        let my hearing,
be for others a small liberation this day.

And let others liberate me by their attention,
when I am locked within.

20 January

Operation

As I pray for my friend who is facing an operation today,
I want to offer thanks:
for anaesthetic,
for antibiotics,
for analgesics,
and for all the products of research that will make this
day not only possible, but also much more
comfortable than it might have been.

I want to pray too for all involved:
for clear-sighted, steady-handed surgeons,
for vigilant anaesthetists,
careful assistants in theatre and
compassionate staff in the recovery ward.

But my heart is with my friend,
so vulnerable today.
Be with (*name*) today.
Keep (*name*) safe.
Make (*name*) well.
Let (*name*) feel loved this day.
Because *she/he* is.

21 January

Treading softly

Abba, creator, you made us dreaming
creatures but left us to puzzle out why.
Help us, as we emerge from the mystery and
chaos of our dream-world, to have some
sense of its significance and meaning, and to make
connections with the dream-world of
others, that we might
tread softly,
discover harmony and
live peacefully with our neighbours,
ourselves and with you,
now and for ever.

22 January

————•◆•————

The undiagnosed

Hear my prayer, this day, for all who await a diagnosis.
For those with unexplained
lumps or mysterious
symptoms.
Those who suddenly lack
energy or who have recently lost
appetite, colour or weight.

I pray for those not sure what their minds
are doing, who wonder whether
their perceptions are real or feelings reliable.

I bring before you any whose
uncertainty about their health
is compounded by deep anxiety.

Give them calm hearts, and guide them
to the wise counsellors, consultants and
healers they need.

23 January

The powerless

Sometimes I realize, when my moments are
enlightened, that my own suffering is
little and small. The plight of others, so often in
view but so rarely taken to heart, scales it
down. This awareness is not a
tactic, not a method to calm my
mind, to put it all in
perspective. That never works.
It's just that my attention has been drawn
away from myself and I've been bent back into
shape, not curved inwards, but reaching
beyond with eyes and arms.

And now another phase, another
challenge, in fact another
agony – the suffering that I will never
see, never know, because it is
hidden, the screams that no one will
hear because they are stifled, or
yowled into thick, disinterested walls.

This hidden suffering fills my prayer
this day; it is my concern, my active distress.

So hear me,
hear me, I say, as I pray
for the powerless poor,
for children of abusive parents,
for aged elders, alone and afraid,
for people with medical conditions too rare to be researched,
for individuals with habits and thoughts that frighten others
    as much as themselves,
for political minorities under ruthless regimes,
for refugees from war zones,
for those who relive the torture of former days.
And all those whose suffering is hidden, unimagined and
shaming of our race.

Give them peace.
Bless them with hope.
Free them from oppression.
Guide them into your place of
    joy and
bind us in the solidarity of your
    loving will
with the one
who escaped hidden suffering,
only to be publicly shamed for the healing
of all.

24 January

The indebted

O God, this New Year is
not looking prosperous at all.
As I review my finances
I see real trouble ahead,
winking at me through the gloom of uncertainty.

Turn Thou this prayer from my anxious
self-interest
to all whose lives are blighted by unpayable
debt.

Be with your children entrapped by
ruthless system or
reckless decision,
and share with all the
untradeable riches of your grace.
Bring us to the eternal home
where debts are dissolved by the
generous forgiveness of others.

25 January (Conversion of St Paul)

Come, Holy Spirit

Come, Holy Spirit,
come this day,
not on my terms,
but yours.

Come as light, as longing,
as love.

Come as light, as longing,
as joy.

Come as light, as longing,
as peace.

Come, Holy Spirit,
come this day,
not on my terms,
but yours.

Come as breath, as wind,
as love.

Come as breath, as wind,
as joy.

Come as breath, as wind,
as peace.

Come, Holy Spirit,
come this day,
not on my terms,
but yours.

26 January

Those burdened by life itself

I am full of life
today, full of energy.

I delight in all I see and
hear. I rejoice in those
around me. I am positive about
my tasks and looking
forward to my challenges and chores.
But my mind goes to those who are
tired of life; my heart goes out to those for whom
living has become a burden they would
prefer to be without; to those who want to die;
to those who want no longer to be.

Be present with them, give them a sense of your
love and mercy, let me be drawn
to their side and give me the confidence
to share their heaviness while remaining
grateful for
my own life – and
theirs.

27 January
(Holocaust Memorial Day)

Darkening the slate

The numbers are surprising.
It is evening, after work,
after school – certainly,
after dark – almost.

The sky remains a luminous slate
but candles are bright.
We expect the usual suspects.
We expect, otherwise, two or three more,
to be gathered together:
a synagogue of sadness, one might say.

The time is planned.
Arrival, movement, welcome, words . . .
We lay stones on a memorial stone.
It's darker already.
And behind their glass the candles are brighter.
There is music – a violin, a voice.
A poem sung cuts the air with skeletal lamentation.
More stones are laid.
The numbers surprise.
A prayer is recited, Kaddish.
The word *shalom* reaches from its heart:
to touch and bind us as one;
to touch and liberate us as many.

The silence congeals.
Transcending the shuffling, the song,
even the restless mind's self-distracting gabble.
Into that silence we tumble
as the slate loses its glow.

Now it is dark.
Now we depart.
A vow has settled in our
broken heart:
never,
never,
never,
again.

Anywhere.

FLOURISHING

What does it mean to flourish?

The word implies health, at least, if not vigour and strength. We flourish when we use our capacities to the full, when we achieve something great without completely exhausting ourselves or wrecking all our relationships.

A good or true community properly seeks the flourishing of all its members, and will not willingly see any diminished.

Flourishing rightly suggests fullness of life, fulfilment, and delight in being active. To flourish is to bloom; to fulfil hidden potential. There is both relief and surprise in flourishing. Relief that some frustration has been vanquished, and surprise that the glorious new whole is so much more than the sum of the previously unintegrated parts.

Flourishing is beautiful – a delight to behold; a wonder to experience. Flourishing brings its own ecstasy. It is so richly, abundantly, entirely complete that it needs to create another dimension. Just as it transcends what seemed like solid limits, so it also transcends itself. And yet to flourish is not to cheat the sharp blade of death or to step outside time, however ecstatic we feel.

We flourish, then, not as those who bloom into eternal completeness, but as those who will continue to plod forward. To flourish is to pause, rather than to stop. Our fulfilment needs its moment and we rightly give way.

And then, a heartbeat later, we begin to move forward in much the same way as before – plodding, falling humankind that we are. Vulnerable to gravity and sin, hurting in the flesh and in frustrated hopes as ever before.

To flourish, then, is not to stop for long. It is certainly not to hold our breath. No, we seek all the more earnestly the breath of spirit and the water of life. We look around us again and respond with envy or thanks to the glories of others. We look, stare, long for the light that will lead us – all of us – home, knowing only that our former flourishing was but a foretaste of the flourishing that is yet to come.

28 January

Way, truth, life

Lord Jesus Christ,
you are the way, the truth and the life.
Help us to continue in the way,
sharing your truth and living life to the full
by emulating your clarity of mind,
generosity of spirit and
obedience to the will of
God, who made us for
love and calls us to fulfilling
service in your name.

29 January

———◆———

The welling

It's not the well,
it's the welling.

It's not the water,
it's the living.

It's not the dying,
it's the rising.

It's not the worship,
it's the truth.

It's not the tradition
or the place:
it's the Spirit;
it's the grace.

30 January

———•◆•———

Thanksgiving

Sometimes I hear of someone whose
life is so impressive that I am
silenced.
Help me to settle into that silence
of admiration with true
humility, and
let it come to fruition in
thanks and praise:
   for those who overcome adversity;
   for those who are unjustly harmed, yet hold no grudge;
   for those whose poverty liberates profound riches;
   for those whose creativity fashions beauty and excellence;
   for those who were once crushed, but now overflow with life;
   for those who encourage others with their resilience and grace;
   for those who never give up, though afflicted by the
         deepest despair;
   for those whose hope is deep, dark and determined;
   for those whose most determined purpose is to give:
   for all these – thanks be to God.

31 January

Let me live well

Lord Jesus Christ,
you promise abundant life to those who
follow you; help me to live this day
to the full.

Let my heart beat slowly.
   Let my breath be deep and regular.
      Let my eyes be attentive and patient.
         Let my stride be even and full of purpose.
            Let my hands be constructive and creative.

Let me live this day as a witness to
your grace,
   your truth,
      your love.
Let me
live well.

1 February

Longing for light

The more I peer, with squinting hope, the
less I see.
Staring into a pupil-black
well, I know water is there.
Drop a stone,
wait,
splash.
I hear the water, but don't see.

Under overcast sky, the stout-black sea
offers not even a hint of a reflection
of my
would-be penetrating gaze.

This is my longing, my thwarted,
humiliated,
restless longing . . .
my soul yearns for responsive depth.
I cast myself into the well.
I hurl myself into the ocean.

No reflection.
No echo.
Nothing.

This isn't the dark night of the soul.
It's the black hole of the spirit.

I want more than anything to abandon my longing.
I cannot: my longing longs,
and I am in the longing,
completely.

Come Thou!
  Come spark!
    Come dawn!
      Come kindly light!

I trust you will come.
I know you will come.
Yet while I squint, stare and gaze
with concentrated intensity,
I know you will appear
elsewhere.
And yet I stare.

2 February (Candlemas)

A sword

We should have seen it coming, but
no one did. Luke's version was so
tidy, a tale of two children,
two mothers, one silent man,
an angel, a walk, a leap and
two songs.
And then a third song, different in
tone: tired and yet fulfilled,
glimpsing the longed-for light
yet seeking escape.
A prelude to a blessing, and in the
blessing we had hoped, assumed,
dared to expect . . .
completion,
closure, perhaps.
Now there's a hope.

How foolish!
　How slow of heart!
　　How self-serving our understanding!

Words come: gnomic, unwelcome.
They speak of
disorder, opposition,
revelation, no less.

We had hoped for a new order.
We are offered a new chaos.
What light is this, but a new darkness?
Enough!

At last it comes. The word that cleaves
the air and stuns us, arresting our
senses and losing Anna's delight in its wake.
After this, her presence – calm itself – is lost
to us.

'There will be a sword.'
A sword, no less.
A sword
through your young soul, young
mother.
I ponder that, as I pray to depart
in peace,
in peace,
in peace.

A prayer before ending

God the Almighty, your son Jesus Christ was presented in the Temple, the child of poor, humble and faithful parents. Inspire us, we pray, to offer ourselves in your loving service with the same humility, that through our lives your grace may be revealed, and by our love of neighbour and enemy your light may shine throughout the world, to your praise and glory, and for the good of all people.